APARTMENT

RENTING

T0196054

BASICS

By Ame Penn

iUniverse, Inc.
New York Bloomington

Dear Reader,

I am writing this book as a guide to you. I have been an Apartment Leasing Specialist for over 10 years and have specialized experience with lease agreements and addendums.

I am not a lawyer or a judge, so for all legal matters pertaining to your future rental home, please seek proper legal counsel.

The entire rental contract you sign is a legal, binding contract and once you sign it you are obligated to it.

Please, do not assume that your family and friends know more than a lawyer does. I have seen residents take wrong advice and end up paying out large sums of money and/or become unable to get another apartment for at least 7 years due to an eviction.

I wish you wonderful, exciting adventures as you begin your journey to independence.

WHEN YOU ARE ENTERING INTO ANY CONTRACT, IF YOU ARE NOT CERTAIN WHAT YOU ARE SIGNING, SEEK LEGAL ASSISTANCE.

- **Ame Penn**

APARTMENT RENTING BASICS
Apartment renting for the novice

iUniverse books may be ordered through booksellers or by contacting:

iUniverse
1663 Liberty Drive
Bloomington, IN 47403
www.iuniverse.com
1-800-Authors (1-800-288-4677)

ISBN: 978-1-4401-2887-5 (pbk)
ISBN: 978-1-4401-2888-2 (ebk)

Printed in the United States of America

iUniverse rev. date: 3/2/2009

What Are The Pros And Cons Of Renting?

Renting an apartment has many benefits, depending on what apartment community you choose.   Some facilities may have a variety of amenities, such as a 24 hour fitness center, sports court, or even a business center included in your rent.

Some everyday hassles can be virtually eliminated by renting. What about a maintenance staff to take care of apartment repairs or a grounds person to mow the lawn?   Keep in mind, though, that while maintenance is a great perk, make sure to keep your precious items put away, to avoid any potential questions, just in case someone needs to come in and out of your home to fix items. This keeps everyone honest and out of trouble.

When placing a work order, make sure you document the date, time, and to whom you gave the work order. Check your lease agreement as there should be a paragraph that shows how long the community maintenance team has to make repairs. If your community management team fails to provide timely maintenance this, could provide an out from your lease agreement.

You will find living in an apartment community has both ups and downs in several areas. You get to pick the community you wish to live in, but you do not get to pick your neighbors.

Remember an apartment community has hundreds of residents, and just as you can see and hear them, they can see and hear you.

Some things to think about when shopping for a possible apartment: can you hear your neighbors' television, radio or voices? Much of this will depend on the quality of the construction of the building.   Unfortunately, it can be like a game of chance since you never fully know what you're going to get until you're living there.

Do not expect complete quiet in an apartment community or any housing where there is shared space. This includes duplexes, dorms or condos. If you do not like noise, it is best to look into renting a house.

One way to break the ice with your neighbors and get to know them is this: when moving in, knock on their door, explaining that you are testing your TV and radio. Ask them to knock on the wall or ceiling if the noise is too loud, as this will give you a basis for your noise levels.

Unfortunately, there are those neighbors who think they are above the rules. There are community rules put in place, in the event that you should encounter noisy, abusive or filthy neighbors. Some neighbors honestly do not realize they are being bothersome.

If you have ongoing problems after you move in that you are unable to resolve with your neighbor, put in writing what is happening and inform your community management team.

If talking to the neighbor doesn't work, your property might have a courtesy patrol you can call to get additional help. If the courtesy patrol is ineffective, contact your local law enforcement agency as they can make most noise and any other violations stop.

Remember to document any complaints with your community management staff. Documentation may get you out of your lease if the community is in violation of the lease agreement. This is not a guarantee that you will get out of your lease, but it can show the ineffectiveness of your community management staff.

Seek a legal counselor when you are uncertain if your rights have been violated. Once again, document what you are reporting, as well as the date, time and to whom you gave the information in the leasing office. Ask them to put a copy of your document in your leasing file. Always cover yourself, even if it seems like everything is and will be going well.

Creating Your Budget

There are many things you need to think about when getting ready to look for your new home. One main starting point is creating a budget. Make sure you can afford the home you are trying to rent.

Do not assume that you can rent anywhere, or that you can qualify. (I will explain qualifying a bit later.)

Your budget should be your top priority. This will set the basis for how much you can afford to rent. *Do not let a quick selling leasing agent talk you into something out of your budget.*

When you are renting, making your rental payment will become the most important payment on the list. A leasing agent's job is not to help you watch your budget. His or her job is to rent units, (and, in most cases, they get a bonus for renting.) They also have rental quota's they must uphold. So: their job is to rent units; yours is to ensure that the home you rent fits into your budget.

What they are offering you may sound great, but if you can afford it for only four months and then are unable to make your payments for the next year, the responsibility doesn't fall on them. It falls 100% on you, and it will affect your credit record and the chance for another apartment later.

You do not need to find your ideal apartment your first time out. Make compromises and keep looking until you get an apartment that you can afford and feel satisfied living in, until you can afford a better place.

In most cases renting an apartment is just a temporary living condition, until something happens like you get "the ultimate job" and must transfer, or you buy a home.

There are also pros and cons of moving from one community to another. The pros: you still have a management team to care for you. Not to mention new neighbors… Oh wait this could be a con!

Be aware of the cost and time it takes for each move. Take your time finding the community that will make you happy, it will pay off in the long run. I have enclosed sample budget sheets. This will give you a guideline as to what you can afford.

Resources to Find Your Home

There are many methods you can use to find your new home. Pounding the pavement and going from apartment to apartment is the time consuming way. It eats up your gas and you may not even qualify for a large percentage of the apartments you spend time touring. There are ways to narrow your search.

Apartment magazines/internet sites: Magazines at your local grocery store have every apartment set in city grids with phone numbers, addresses, the amenities offered, their pet policies and, sometimes, pricing or specials.

With these resources, you can easily find the apartments that interest you, call ahead and make an appointment with a Leasing Specialist. If you wish to see a photo view of the property first, the internet addresses of most of the properties are also usually listed in the magazines. You might also find a special on the apartment's web site.

Local locator services: Most of the locator services rely on commissions for referring clients to the community that he or she rents from. This means this service should be free to you. The locator service will contact a community for you, getting up-to-date pricing or specials. They also have lists of what amenities the property will offer to you. All you need to do is let them know what amenities you'd like, your price range and any special needs you have.

The locator service will give you a list of communities which would best fit your needs, based on the information you provide. Remember to give the community the name of your locator service when you visit.

It is also nice to contact the locator service letting them know what community you are moving into and when you are moving. Again, they are paid by the community you are moving into.

Newspapers: Newspaper advertisements outline rental homes in your area. They give a description of the home, pet, smoking policies, and pricing. Rental houses can be good for those who have bad credit, criminal records, or hate the thought of having 300 hundred plus neighbors all in one space.

Qualify For the Apartment

Oh, you didn't know you must be able to "qualify"? Yes, apartment communities have lists of what they are looking for in tenants.

There are questions you must ask the leasing person:

1. **Ask to see their community qualification outline.** This will give you an understanding of what you will need to qualify. With Fair Housing laws, most communities should have an outline. For those who do not carry an outline, then ask the following questions:

2. **How old must you be to qualify?** Some apartment communities have a policy that you must be 18 years and older to rent, while others require renters to be 21 years and over.

Senior Living Communities may have a policy that all residents must be around 36 years or older, depending on their community's policy.

3. **How many people can live in a home**? This will let you know if you might have two people next door or twelve.

The state you live in should have an outline of how many people per rental home are allowed in the state. Keep in mind that the state's guideline may be higher than what an actual apartment community allows. For example, if the state allows five people in a two bedroom unit, but the apartment community only wishes to allow three people in a two bedroom unit, the community policy will help with Fair Housing policies, due to treating all residents equally.

4. **How long do I have to be at a job and how much do I need to make to qualify?** Depending on the community you choose, they may require you be at your job for at least one year prior to renting.

Some communities want your monthly income to be at least 1.5 times the amount of market rent. Some apartment communities require your monthly income to be at least two or even three times the amount of market rent. Find out, so you know whether or not this is a community you can even consider.

5. **Ask your leasing person if you are qualifying on market rent or discounted rent.**

For example, if you make $2000 a month and your rent is $800, at market then you qualify at 2.5 times the rent amount. However, if you make $2000 with a discounted rent of $650, you will qualify at 3 times the amount of rent.

"Market rent" is the rent the community would normally get if no discount was offered.

$_____ (what you make) divided by the rent rate $_____ = _____ qualifying rate.

6. **What kind of rental history will I need to qualify?**

The community may wish that you have at least one year of rental history or have lived in a college dorm or military dorm for at least one year to qualify.

If you have had an apartment and can show you were never late with your rental payments, this will help with your qualification.

If you were ever late you may be required to pay an additional deposit or you may not qualify at all. This will depend on how many late payments you made in a year or in your lease term. Again, this should be outlined in the community rental policy.

7. **What is the deposit amount if you qualify? What would it be if you needed an extra deposit? For what reasons would an extra deposit be required?**

Each community has their own deposit pricing and qualifications for an extra deposit. Ask for the rental policy outline again this will guide you into your qualifications.

Co-signer or a Guarantor?

If you want to live in the community but can't qualify under their terms, ask if you could have a Co-signer or a Guarantor.

Co-signer
This is a parent or guardian who will guarantee that they will make your rental payment if you are unable to. This person will be placed on your rental agreement as a lease holder and, in most cases; the community management will give keys to your unit and information about you to the co-signer.

Guarantor
This is a parent or guardian who is willing to place in writing a guarantee to assume your rental payment if, for some reason, you cannot make your rental payments. This person will not be entered on your lease as a lease holder, but will sign a separate guarantor form.

This will not allow the person or persons to have access to your home or give them the ability to make changes to any portion of your leasing agreement.

A co-signer and/or guarantor, is responsible to pay the rent if you are unable to do so.

By not paying your rent on time, you could destroy the credit record of the person who is helping you. Let them know immediately if you will be unable to make your rental payment. *Do not wait until you are already late on your rent payment.*

If you are evicted due to either party not making the payment, the eviction will show on your credit record and theirs.

I would advise that either party think twice before being either a Co-signer or a guarantor, prior to signing any lease.

Should You Have a Roommate?

A roommate can be great to help share in your cost of living. However, you'll need to consider possible pitfalls. What if they lose their job and can't provide their portion of the rent?

By entering in the lease agreement with another person, you are agreeing to pay the rent: all of it. It needs to be paid, on time, in full, every month. The apartment management doesn't care who is paying the rent as long as it is paid in full. So the question is: can you make the entire rent if you need to, so it doesn't affect your credit?

Can you easily kick your roommate out? No, you would need to go to court. You both entered into a lease contract that is a legal binding contract.

What if your roommate is filthy, steals your items, or brings home a houseguest to stay for prolonged periods of time? The best thing to do is address potential problems ahead of time.

House rules set up boundaries ahead of time and should not be looked at lightly.   You and your roommate should write out all of your expectations of each other before ever considering signing a lease together.

In a roommate situation, everyone should have a lock on his or her own bedroom door for their personal privacy. Do remember to give any extra keys to bedroom doors to your apartment management staff, in case of an emergency. If there is an emergency and they have to drill the lock to the doors there will be an accrued expense that you will have to pay, so plan ahead.

When you put in locking door knobs, be sure to save the original doorknobs that came with the apartment. When you move out, replace the original knobs that came with the apartment. You must return the apartment to the same condition that it was in when you moved in.

Remember, unless your roommate is becoming threatening, unruly or stealing, the police in most cases will not get involved in roommate disputes.

So what should you do with a roommate for non-payment? Have the leasing person photocopy your checks and have them sign and date the copies. (Actually, you should do this even if you do not have a roommate.)

This will show the date, time, and to whom you paid your rent each month. If the property sold to a new owner, or if something went wrong with the computer system or accounting system, this will show your payments.

Keep these copies in a filing cabinet along with your lease copy and any correspondence to and from the community, whether or not you choose to have a roommate.

If you need to, you can use the receipts in court to show your willingness to pay and your roommate's non-willingness to pay. Remember, I am not a lawyer or a judge, but covering yourself is always a good idea. If you have to go to court over non-payment, a judge might decide on restitution on your behalf if you have appropriate documentation.

If you have a difficult or non-paying roommate, talking with your property manager is also a good idea. Some management companies are willing to put you in a smaller home so you can get rid of the deadbeat. Overall, that would be a win-win situation for all parties involved.

Be prepared: during the term of your lease, the friend you had for years and then made your roommate might not be a friend by the end of the lease.

Pets

Are you planning to bring any pets along to your new home?

Most communities will allow one to two pets, but there are also communities that do not allow pets at all. If you must have a pet, ask the leasing agent if they allow pets before you sign an agreement.

Most communities will require renters' insurance for pet owners in case the pet decides to explore its wild side. Cats and dogs can both cause damage to people and property. Sometimes this happens because an animal feels threatened by a maintenance person or if they feel they are protecting their home.

Another consideration: Most communities have breed and pet restrictions. Does your pet meet the community's qualifications?

Most communities will not allow any animals other than cats or dogs. That means no ferrets, rabbits, lizards or snakes. Some communities will require renters' insurance for residents who want to have a fish tank. Talk with your leasing agent about insurance pertaining to pets at your complex.

Do not think you can outsmart your community management team by bringing in a restricted breed or pet. In most states, depending on how the lease reads, they can enter into your apartment to do a health and welfare check. This check could occur within minutes of determining you have a pet, or up to 72 hours depending on the lease, state and federal laws.

There is always the possibility of an emergency maintenance need and you're not home: BUSTED! In most lease agreements they can call animal control and have your unlawful pet removed from your home, although some communities will give a couple of days' notice to remove the forbidden pet. There are communities who have a zero tolerance for non compliant residents and may just evict for the pet infraction.

The infraction will be listed in your leasing file. When it is time to renew your lease, in most states, the community management team can decide to not renew. When it is time for you to get a new apartment, this infraction also could affect you not getting approved for a new home as well.

Think twice about breaking the community rules and violating your lease. It may not seem like a big deal to you, but it is to the community management team. An eviction can cost you the ability to rent an apartment for at least seven years.

What about an Service Animal?

To be considered a Service Animal, the animal must be certified by a doctor or the state and have its papers showing its designation as a Service Animal. Just because you say it is a guide dog doesn't make it one.

Check with **www.HUD.gov.** HUD has a link to The Fair Housing and Equal Opportunity (FHEO) site. The FHEO has a great outline to help you understand your rights regarding Service Animals, and options to pursue if you feel those rights have been violated.

Exceptions to the rules are certified companions or guide dogs. Certified Service Animals are not considered "pets."

What You Will Need in Your Search

I have enclosed a few forms to help you as you are looking around. These will help you with building your property checklists of: who, what, how, why and when.

It is very important to ask questions and keep good notes. After the first couple of properties, the communities will start looking the same, so it is important to have an idea of what communities you visited and what communities you liked or disliked.

What you will need to bring with you on your first trip to a property:

1. <u>Apartment Stat Sheet:</u> Make a copy for every property you plan to visit. This will keep everything in order. If you do not like the property, do not keep the form, as it will add to your confusion.

2. <u>Property Amenities Sheet:</u> This sheet will help you keep notes about all the amenities a property offers. Just circle what amenities the property has.

3. <u>Measuring Tape:</u> Bring one that is at least 30 feet long. It may sound odd, I know, but wouldn't you want to make sure the bedroom set you just bought really can fit? Measure your furniture prior to viewing homes. This will put you ahead of the game.

4. <u>Your ID:</u> Almost all communities require proper identification to show units for everyone 18 years of age and older. Your ID is a must. It is policy that you must give it to the agent for holding. There are bad people with ill intentions, so this is not personal; this is keeping the leasing agents safety in mind.

5. <u>Pay Stubs and other information:</u> Just in case you decide you want to apply for a property, pay stubs will help fast-track your application process. Also bring phone numbers and addresses of past properties from which you have rented. Bring your employment information, including your boss's direct telephone line. Keep in mind that if you have a 900 number, most of the communities use third party services and they are unable to verify by the 900 number, so a regular telephone number is essential. The more information you can provide on your past jobs and rental history, the more this will help expedite your rental process.

I also advise you to bring your check book, just in case you like a property and know it is the one you must have. However, keep in mind that many communities may require a money order (rather than a personal check) for the application fee and another for the deposit. Yes: two money orders or cashier checks. Due to high volumes of monies coming through a property at anyone time, communities do not allow cash.

The application fee is non-refundable, although, in most cases, the deposit may be refundable. Get in writing how long the deposit is refundable for, and for what reasons would it be non-refundable. If you lie on your application, that is fraud and, in most states, it will be an automatic loss of your deposit. *DO NOT LIE ON YOUR APPLICATION.*

Making Your Move Easier

Now that you have found your home, been accepted and paid the required fees, you should have received your welcome letter from your community. This will have your new address and what payments you will need to make prior to moving in.

Seeing your home before signing for it:
Did you get to see your future home? If not… "Ouch!" I hope it is to your liking. I would not rent from a community unless I could see my physical home first, so I strongly recommend making that part of the initial search and acceptance process.

Perhaps they gave you the excuse that, "It wasn't ready yet." Or maybe they showed you a model. Um no, I would keep looking. You want to see your home so you know what you are signing up for!

I have seen the nightmares of not seeing an apartment first. I did a move across country, with my family, sight unseen, and found out I was lied to. No A/C, it was a window unit and the apartment was built in the early 1900's. I was then stuck in a lease I was legally bound to for 12 months. Yes, I could have fought it, but the time and money wasn't worth it. I took it as a lesson learned.

What if you are allergic to pets and the past resident had them? Just imagine what you could be getting yourself into!

Remember to ask what the utility phone numbers are, so you can have them set up prior to move-in. This will eliminate a lot of your stress prior to your move day. I have enclosed worksheets for the utility companies to help you get ready.

You can contact the utility companies a couple of days or weeks in advance to have this done. When you call, ask each company what the approximate usage was by the past resident and what the average cost could be. This will help with your budgeting and eliminate unpleasant surprises.

Do not forget that there is a rate increase about once a year (or more) for water, sewage, gas and electricity. Do not assume what the past renter paid will be the same price you will pay. Always add extra to your budget to be safe.

Move-In Day

1. **Money order/ Online Pay/ Checkbook:** Ask the leasing agent ahead of time how you can pay your move-in cost.

Most require money orders or cashier checks. However, there are communities which have web sites to pay online (for a fee.) Some communities may let you still pay by personal check as well. Remember: NO CASH.

Do not forget your receipt. This is your proof of payment. Always get a receipt when you pay your rent: every month!

Ask the leasing person to copy your personal check, money order, and/or cashier's check and sign the copy. Another alternative is to have them sign the carbon copy of your personal check. Either way, you need a date, time and to whom you gave it. There are times checks get misplaced or thrown away by accident. Remember that it is your responsibility to cover yourself.

2. **Utilities:** Be sure to have your utilities turned on before you move. This will save you time and it will make your move less stressful.

3. **Two Day Survival Kit:** Pack a kit of the household items that will get you through for the first two days of your move. This will keep you from hunting down boxes, save time, and reduce stress.

Put these boxes in a closet and place a sign on the door that says, "Two Day Survival Kit." I have enclosed one in this book for you, along with the list of what you may need for the first two days.

4. **Phone List:** This is a list your leasing agent should have of area, schools, hospitals, DMV, delivery places, and their numbers, as well as non-emergency numbers for the community. Place on your refrigerator for safe keeping.

5. **File:** This is the file you should have created when you placed your deposit and application fee down. This file should have the name of the community on it and date of move-in along with a stapled business card of your Leasing Specialist.

It should also contain the welcome sheet, the move-in cost sheet, copies of your deposit and application fees. This file should be used for all documentation and work orders you place, future payments and correspondence with the community.

6. **<u>Apartment Move-in Checklist:</u>** This will be provided by your management staff. Go through the apartment before moving in and mark all flaws you see. Be sure to include the cleaning of the home, scratches, dings, stains, holes and chips on *everything*. Do not walk through and say all is OK. This could be a costly mistake. They will use this checklist when you move out. If there is any damage not listed on the move-in sheet, you will be responsible for all damages, regardless if you had caused them.

When you do your move-in checklist, take pictures with time and date stamps of the apartment and staple them to your copy of the checklist. Do not just hand it over to the community management team. Always keep copies.

Ask about light bulbs and nail holes. Who is responsible for light bulbs? Get it in writing. Who fixes nail holes? If you assume it will be the community's responsibility, you may pay extra at move out.

The checklist should be done prior to moving in. Take a half hour and go through the home. Do check everywhere, even behind the washer, the dryer, and the vents. Do not assume it was done. Things do get missed, during the make ready.

7. **<u>Work Order List:</u>** This is everything you found wrong that needs repair. You are renting an apartment that probably has had five or more past residents. Do not expect everything (or anything) to be new. Even a brand new apartment community has nicks and scratches, so do not expect everything to be perfect.

Work orders are for things like: blinds not working, toilet running, alarms not working, locks and latches not working, refrigerator not cold enough, dryer vent not connected, washer hoses not connected, no filter for the furnace or leaks under sinks. These are just a few items that could be wrong.

Ask to have a maintenance staff member show you how to do minor repairs. They can give you the dos and don'ts of your home to help with quick-fix tips. This leads me into Number 8:

8. **Trouble Shooting Guide:** There are several things that you will need to know about your new home to avoid problems.

Ask your leasing agent:

Do they have a guide of what not to put in your garbage disposal (if you have one)?

Does the property provide a Carbon Monoxide Detector? If not, buy one, if gas is being used in your apartment.

Who takes care of the air filter for your heater?
How should you change your air filter? If it is your responsibility, mark a place on your calendar for a reminder to replace your filter. It should be changed every three months (or sooner) depending how quickly it gets dirty. The cleaner the filter is, the better your heating unit will run.

How do you reset your GFI or circuit breakers?
Ask your maintenance staff to show you where your GFI is located. If some of your apartment lights go out, instead of your circuit breaker going out, it could be your GFI. The GFI is your power surge protector, generally outlets near water, such as a bathroom. If a blow dryer was to fall into your sink, it would trip the GFI and turn off the power so you would not get electrocuted.

How do you use a plunger?
Let's talk about the plunger for a moment. It should be your responsibility to own one. You should make an attempt to remove the item that could be causing your back up.

There are times even a plunger doesn't work. For example, what happens if an action figure makes his way down the chute? This would be one of those times you should call maintenance to come use a metal snake to retrieve the item. Be aware: depending on the community this may cost you for the wrong items being placed down your toilet.

What is defined as an emergency work order?
Could it be only having one toilet which is backed up? Perhaps your electricity is going out, or your alarms keep chirping and you need to sleep. Find out ahead of time what they expect.

Why Rental Insurance?

What is rental insurance? It is your personal property insurance if you are faced with an unforeseen emergency such as fire, flood, burglary, environmental problems, water leaks, ice or lightning just to name a few. Your landlord's insurance does not cover your belongings! It only covers the building itself. Taking care of your things is your responsibility, and it is very, very important.

Relative to the cost of coverage, renters' insurance is a great buy. Don't say you can't afford it. You can't afford not to have it! Rather than spending a few extra dollars on lattes or a community with a sauna, invest that money in your protection.

When meeting with your rental insurance company, make sure you know what your deductible is. This is an amount you must pay prior to getting your money for the loss of your personal items. For example, if you have a fire and it is determined that you lost $1500 worth of items, and you have a $500 deductible, you would receive $1000 from the insurance company. Generally, the higher your deducible is, the lower your premiums are.

There are many ways to save money on insurance:

- Ask about discounts for signing up for auto insurance with the same company.
- Ask if the company you work for is on their preferred employer program.
- Ask about discounts for deadbolt locks, alarms, and non-smoker discounts, if everyone in your household is a non-smoker.
- Ask the agent what other benefits you get with this policy.
- If you are robbed on vacation does your renters' insurance cover your loss?
- Does the insurance cover liability, in case a guest gets hurt in your home?
- Do they offer discounts for a pet-free home?

Finally, ask the insurance agent, for a list of questions you will need to ask your property management. Your agent will need this information to give you an accurate quote and correctly write the policy.

- How far is the nearest fire station?
- Are there approved fire doors?
- Where are fire alarms and extinguishers located?
- Is your building wood framed or concrete?

These are just a few of the questions you need to ask.

Renter's insurance can be inexpensive: as low as $10 per month (or more) depending on how much insurance you may need. The more insurance you need, the more you'll pay, but it is well worth the cost. If you have $15,000 in computer equipment, plasmas TVs and stereos don't go for a cheap policy that only covers $5,000. Overall, it's very inexpensive to cover the thousands it may cost to replace your belongings. The amount you pay is based on how much coverage you will need, along with any discounts the company may offer.

Shop around; don't just talk to one insurance agent. You might be surprised at the wide variety in costs and coverage. Be an informed consumer!

When you have your policy in place and move in, as soon as possible, take pictures of all your high end belongings, make a copy of your receipt and staple it to the picture. This will give you the date of purchase along with its actual cost. This includes your bedroom furniture, TV, radio, art work and collectables. Do not staple the receipt, the ink fades after a few months and makes it hard to prove your purchase.

If you have a video camera, go through your entire apartment and videotape everything: contents of closets, drawers, etc. If your home burns down, you will have to give the adjuster a list of everything that was lost, and be able to prove that you actually owned the items. Could you really do all that from memory?

It is wise to invest in a small fireproof safe for these documents, as well as for your social security card, birth certificate, car title, and any other important papers.

What happens if your refrigerator goes out and you lose all your food? This is an unforeseen act and can be covered by your insurance. Yes, I understand that it is their refrigerator, but it is your food.

What happens if your car is broken into on the property?
Your auto insurance will cover any damages or losses within their policy guidelines. The apartment community is not responsible for this, either. Crime happens and, unfortunately, you may be the one to whom it happens.

If you leave personal belongings in your car, you are asking for trouble. There is no such thing as a crime free neighborhood.

Check with your local law enforcement agency to see the property crime statistics for your community. Most law enforcement agencies, can give you readouts, of what crimes were committed in the area you wish to live and the surrounding community. This can help you in your decision about where to live.

The best advocate for you is your insurance company; they know the rules and can help with all your questions.

Moving Out of Your Community

1. **Notice to Vacate:** This is common sense, but always put in writing, you are giving notice to vacate; make sure you are giving the proper notification. (Check your lease for what kind of notice you need to give and how far in advance!)

   Near the end of your lease term, you may receive a notice to renew your contract from your community management team. However, in most states it is not required to give you a notice. Your lease contract is your notice of renewal. (This is another good reason to read it closely and keep a copy of it!)

   Many communities however, give notice of renewal as a courtesy to you. When you receive your renewal letter, this would be the time to give your notice, of not renewing your lease agreement.

   Make sure you put in writing the date, time, and get a signature from the leasing agent to whom you gave it. Make sure they give you a copy of the notice.

   Place this in the leasing folder you created when you moved into the community. I have seen notices not make it into the residents leasing folder. Your copy of the notice will cover you, if you have to go to court. Another reason to get signature of the person you handed it to.

   Other wise, without the notice you could be placed on a month-to-month lease and most likely pay a higher rent until the notice is fulfilled?

   Without your copy of the notice, do not assume you would win if you went to court!

   Cover yourself by getting and keeping copies of all documentation.

2. **Cleaning:** Make sure you give back your apartment in the condition you received it when you moved in. This is where you need the checklist you had at move-in, where you listed everything that was wrong with your home.

   It should have made it into your community leasing folder in the office, but if it didn't, you'll have your copy. With that, you can focus on cleaning, and not on the items that were listed at move-in.

If you moved in and there were no stains on the carpet, contact the community management team and find out who they use as a carpet cleaner. They are usually cheaper than someone you just find out of the phone book. If you dropped wine or candle wax that would not come up, the stains will cost you. Did you have a pet? If yes, you may be paying for the entire carpet replacement if your pet had an accident in your home. Be prepared to avoid surprises.

Some communities require residents to have carpets professionally cleaned upon move-out and provide a receipt as proof.

If you are too busy or lazy to clean, getting a maid service can be a great way to get things done so you can focus on your new home. Get the cleaning checklist from your community management team. This will give the maid service a guide to go off of.

Ask about light bulbs. Some communities require you to replace all blown out bulbs prior to move-out. You used them, so you need to replace them.

3. **Pre Walk-Through:** When you think everything is out of your home, do a final walk-through of your old home, just to be sure.

Open every cabinet door, the washer and dryer, closet doors, drawers, and the dishwasher. If you have a water heater or a heater unit, check those closets also. Leave the doors open so you know you have checked those areas for any forgotten items. It would be sad to leave your grandmother's antique gravy dish behind.

4. **Management Walk-Through:** Do a walk-through with a manager making sure anything that may have been missed can be fixed before you hand over your keys.

Make sure you get in writing what you would owe, if anything, at the time you checked out with the manager.

If you leave and do not do a walk through, make sure you have kept all your receipts for any professional cleaning services you used. If you need to go to court over bogus charges, this will help you in court. Take pictures of your move-out, making sure there is a date/time stamp on the photos.

5. **Utilities:** Make sure you turn off all your utilities, otherwise the next tenants will get to have their electric, cable and phone services paid for by you. If you saved the utility worksheet I created, it should save you time looking up the phone numbers.

6. **Carbon Monoxide Detector:** Re-invest in a new one when moving into your new home. Do not forget to change them out every 6 months, making sure they keep working effectively. Only buy them if you have gas being used in your home.

Review

Let's recap:

- Before signing an agreement:
    - Are you ready to move and can you make your lease payments?
    - Is it worth having a roommate, or should you live by yourself?
    - If you can't qualify for the community where you want to live, could you have a co-signer or a guarantor?
- Ask lots of questions. A leasing agent isn't a mind reader. They need to know what your needs and price ranges are.
- Always check with your Community Management Team to make sure whether pets are allowed. What kind of pets you can have, what weight and how many? What extra costs and regulations are involved? Remember, if you use a Certified Service Animal, there are special provisions for this.
- Read your lease from front to back. Take your time and seek legal help if you do not understand anything in it. (Don't take the agent's word for anything questionable. Get an actual legal opinion!) The lease agreement is a legally binding contract.
- Purchase a Carbon Monoxide Detector if gas is used in your apartment.
- Get renters' insurance to cover any losses from unforeseen emergencies.
- Connecting and disconnecting your utilities is your responsibility. If you fail to do so, someone else will reap the rewards of your failure to be responsible.
- Make your own leasing file and keep all copies and pictures in that folder.
- Always cover yourself by making copies of your contract, move-in checklist, any checks or money orders, handwritten work orders, complaints against other residents and, most of all, your Notice to Vacate.
- Make sure you get a time, date and signature of the leasing agent of everything you give them. Do not assume the items you gave them will make it into your residential files. Things do get misplaced; to error is human.
- Do not think you are above the rules of the Community. This could cost you a non-renewal or eviction. 7 years is a long time before qualifying for another apartment.
- Always do a walk-through checklist when you move in and do a walk-through with your management team when moving out.

BUDGET WORK SHEET

How much you make monthly really does matter when it comes to renting a home!

Rent	$_____
Phone/Cell	$_____
Electric	$_____
Gas	$_____
W/S/T	$_____ water, sewage and trash
Insurance	$_____
Car Gas	$_____
Renters' Ins	$_____
Credit Card	$_____
Cable	$_____
Food	$_____
_____	$_____
_____	$_____
_____	$_____
=	
	$ _____

After you create your budget, you will need to know what it will cost to move into your future home.

I have created Property Stat Sheet which will give you a breakdown of your costs for move-in.

Utility Companies Work Sheet

Water/Sewage Company? (___) ____-____ _____. Is it individually
metered, divided between residents, or included in rent?

 Monthly Approx Cost $_____

Trash Company? (___) ____-____ _____. Is it individually
billed, divided between residents, or included in rent?

 Monthly Approx Cost $_____

Electric Company? (___) ____-____ _____. Is it individually
metered, divided between residents, or included in rent?

 Monthly Approx Cost $_____

Gas Company? (___) ____-____ _____. Is it individually
metered, divided between residents, or included in rent?

 Monthly Approx Cost $_____

Cable/Dish? (___) ____-____ _____. Is it individually
billed, divided between residents, or included in rent?

 Monthly Approx Cost $_____

Phone Company? (___) ____-____ _____. Is it individually
billed or divided between residents?

 Monthly Approx Cost $_____

You can get an estimate of the utilities by talking with the electric, water and gas companies. They should have what the past tenant used during their lease term. This will help with your budget. Remember, though, with cost increases, you can expect to probably pay a little more than a prior tenant did, but this can give you an estimate.

BUDGET WORK SHEET

How much you make monthly really does matter when it comes to renting a home!

Rent	$_____
Phone/Cell	$_____
Electric	$_____
Gas	$_____
W/S/T	$_____ water, sewage and trash
Insurance	$_____
Car Gas	$_____
Renters' Ins	$_____
Credit Card	$_____
Cable	$_____
Food	$_____
_____	$_____
_____	$_____
_____	$_____
=	
	$ _____

Utility Companies Work Sheet

Water/Sewage Company? (____) _____ - _____ _____. Is it individually
metered, divided between residents, or included in rent?

                                                Monthly Approx Cost $_____

Trash Company? (____) _____ - _____ _____. Is it individually
billed, divided between residents, or included in rent?

                                                Monthly Approx Cost $_____

Electric Company? (____) _____ - _____ _____. Is it individually
metered, divided between residents, or included in rent?

                                                Monthly Approx Cost $_____

Gas Company? (____) _____ - _____ _____. Is it individually
metered, divided between residents, or included in rent?

                                                Monthly Approx Cost $_____

Cable/Dish? (____) _____ - _____ _____. Is it individually
billed, divided between residents, or included in rent?

                                                Monthly Approx Cost $_____

Phone Company? (____) _____ - _____ _____. Is it individually
billed or divided between residents?

                                                Monthly Approx Cost $_____

You can get an estimate of the utilities by talking with the electric, water and gas companies. They should have what the past tenant used during their lease term. This will help with your budget. Remember, though, with cost increases, you can expect to probably pay a little more than a prior tenant did, but this can give you an estimate.

BUDGET WORK SHEET

How much you make monthly really does matter when it comes to renting a home!

Rent	$_____
Phone/Cell	$_____
Electric	$_____
Gas	$_____
W/S/T	$_____ water, sewage and trash
Insurance	$_____
Car Gas	$_____
Renters' Ins	$_____
Credit Card	$_____
Cable	$_____
Food	$_____
_____	$_____
_____	$_____
_____	$_____
=	$ _____

Utility Companies Work Sheet

Water/Sewage Company? (____) _____ - _____ _____ . Is it individually
metered, divided between residents, or included in rent?

            Monthly Approx Cost $_____

Trash Company? (____) _____ - _____ _____ . Is it individually
billed, divided between residents, or included in rent?

            Monthly Approx Cost $_____

Electric Company? (____) _____ - _____ _____ . Is it individually
metered, divided between residents, or included in rent?

            Monthly Approx Cost $_____

Gas Company? (____) _____ - _____ _____ . Is it individually
metered, divided between residents, or included in rent?

            Monthly Approx Cost $_____

Cable/Dish? (____) _____ - _____ _____ . Is it individually
billed, divided between residents, or included in rent?

            Monthly Approx Cost $_____

Phone Company? (____) _____ - _____ _____ . Is it individually
billed or divided between residents?

            Monthly Approx Cost $_____

You can get an estimate of the utilities by talking with the electric, water and gas companies. They should have what the past tenant used during their lease term. This will help with your budget. Remember, though, with cost increases, you can expect to probably pay a little more than a prior tenant did, but this can give you an estimate.

BUDGET WORK SHEET

How much you make monthly really does matter when it comes to renting a home!

Rent	$_____
Phone/Cell	$_____
Electric	$_____
Gas	$_____
W/S/T	$_____ water, sewage and trash
Insurance	$_____
Car Gas	$_____
Renters' Ins	$_____
Credit Card	$_____
Cable	$_____
Food	$_____
_____	$_____
_____	$_____
_____	$_____
=	
	$ _____

Utility Companies Work Sheet

Water/Sewage Company? ( ) _____ - _____ _____ . Is it individually
metered, divided between residents, or included in rent?

        Monthly Approx Cost $_____

Trash Company? ( ) _____ - _____ _____ . Is it individually
billed, divided between residents, or included in rent?

        Monthly Approx Cost $_____

Electric Company? ( ) _____ - _____ _____ . Is it individually
metered, divided between residents, or included in rent?

        Monthly Approx Cost $_____

Gas Company? ( ) _____ - _____ _____ . Is it individually
metered, divided between residents, or included in rent?

        Monthly Approx Cost $_____

Cable/Dish? ( ) _____ - _____ _____ . Is it individually
billed, divided between residents, or included in rent?

        Monthly Approx Cost $_____

Phone Company? ( ) _____ - _____ _____ . Is it individually
billed or divided between residents?

        Monthly Approx Cost $_____

You can get an estimate of the utilities by talking with the electric, water and gas companies. They should have what the past tenant used during their lease term. This will help with your budget. Remember, though, with cost increases, you can expect to probably pay a little more than a prior tenant did, but this can give you an estimate.

Apartment Stat Sheet

YES   NO

Name of Apartment _____

Phone (**)** _____ - _____   **Fax (**   **)** _____ - _____

Address _____

_____

Leasing Person's Name _____

How long are the leases?   MTM   3   4   5   6   7   8   9   10   11   12   13   14   15   16   17   18

Type _____ **Sq Ft** _____ **$** _____   **Type** _____ **Sq Ft** _____ **$** _____

Type _____ **Sq Ft** _____ **$** _____   **Type** _____ **Sq Ft** _____ **$** _____

Type _____ **Sq Ft** _____ **$** _____   **Type** _____ **Sq Ft** _____ **$** _____

Type _____ **Sq Ft** _____ **$** _____   **Type** _____ **Sq Ft** _____ **$** _____

Deposit $** _____ **Non Refundable Admin Fee$ _____ **Application Fee$** _____

Pet Deposit $ _____ **Non Refundable Pet Fee $** _____ **Pet Rent $** _____

Do they allow dogs? _____ **Do they allow cats?** _____ **What size?** _____ **How many?** _____

Does your pet qualify?   Y   N   **Exotic animals allowed?**   Y   N

___ Free Parking   ___Uncovered   ___ Carport   ___ Closed-in Garage   ___ Garage Space

___ Street Parking   ___Paid Lot Parking   **Monthly Cost $** _____

What are the utilities? What do you pay for?

____Water   ___Sewage   ___Trash   ___Electric   ___Gas   ___Cable/Dish TV   ___ Phone

It is your responsibility to connect and disconnect your utilities. Be sure to ask which utilities you should place in your name. *Do not rely on your leasing person to make sure this gets done.* There could be a deposit to pay; the companies could pull your credit record again, although your utilities themselves will not be counted as credit. When you disconnect any service, ask for letters stating your payment history. Some companies in the future may use these letters so you might avoid a deposit another time.

Property Amenities Form

Circle the amenities the property offers

What amenities are offered in the community?

Tennis Court	Basketball Court	Sports Court	Handball Court
Volleyball Court	Swimming Pool	Hot Tub	Sauna
Steam Room	Yoga	Free Weights	Fitness Center
Massage Room	Dance Classes	Walking/Jogging Track	Theater Room
Daycare	Club House	Playground	Fire Pit
Tanning Bed	Barbecue Grills	Casino Trips	Concierge Service
Pet Walking Service	Personal Shopping	Dry Cleaning Service	Grocery Delivery

What amenities are in the home?

Fireplace	A/C	Self Cleaning Oven	Ice Maker
Microwave	DSL/T1 Cable	Stove	Fridge
Dishwasher	Garden Tub	Stand-In Shower	Tub/Shower Combo
Walk-In Closet	Standard Closet	King Size Bedroom	Queen Size Bedroom
Computer Desk	Study	ADA compliant	Crown Molding
Gourmet Kitchen	Granite Counter Tops	Stainless Steel Appliances	Accent Walls

What activities are close to the apartment?

Light Rail	Bus Stop	Shopping	Night Life
Library	Arts	Hobby Shop	Movie Theater
Dance Classes	Fitness	Bakeries	Walking Trails
Camping	Boating	Sports Arenas	Parks
Skating	Skiing	Biking	Fishing

Apartment Stat Sheet

YES   NO

Name of Apartment _____

Phone (   ) _____ - _____   Fax (   ) _____ - _____

Address _____

_____

Leasing Person's Name_____

How long are the leases?   MTM   3   4   5   6   7   8   9   10   11   12   13   14   15   16   17   18

Type _____ Sq Ft _____ $_____   Type _____ Sq Ft _____ $_____

Type _____ Sq Ft _____ $_____   Type _____ Sq Ft _____ $_____

Type _____ Sq Ft _____ $_____   Type _____ Sq Ft _____ $_____

Type _____ Sq Ft _____ $_____   Type _____ Sq Ft _____ $_____

Deposit $ _____ Non Refundable Admin Fee$ _____ Application Fee$_____

Pet Deposit $ _____ Non Refundable Pet Fee $ _____ Pet Rent $_____

Do they allow dogs? _____ Do they allow cats? _____ What size? _____ How many? _____

Does your pet qualify?   Y   N   Exotic animals allowed?   Y   N

___ Free Parking   ___Uncovered   ___ Carport   ___ Closed-in Garage   ___ Garage Space

___ Street Parking   ___Paid Lot Parking   Monthly Cost $_____

What are the utilities? What do you pay for?

____Water   ___Sewage   ___Trash   ___Electric   ___Gas   ___Cable/Dish TV   ___Phone

It is your responsibility to connect and disconnect your utilities. Be sure to ask which utilities you should place in your name. *Do not rely on your leasing person to make sure this gets done.* There could be a deposit to pay; the companies could pull your credit record again, although your utilities themselves will not be counted as credit. When you disconnect any service, ask for letters stating your payment history. Some companies in the future may use these letters so you might avoid a deposit another time.

Property Amenities Form

Circle the amenities the property offers

What amenities are offered in the community?

Tennis Court	Basketball Court	Sports Court	Handball Court
Volleyball Court	Swimming Pool	Hot Tub	Sauna
Steam Room	Yoga	Free Weights	Fitness Center
Massage Room	Dance Classes	Walking/Jogging Track	Theater Room
Daycare	Club House	Playground	Fire Pit
Tanning Bed	Barbecue Grills	Casino Trips	Concierge Service
Pet Walking Service	Personal Shopping	Dry Cleaning Service	Grocery Delivery

What amenities are in the home?

Fireplace	A/C	Self Cleaning Oven	Ice Maker
Microwave	DSL/T1 Cable	Stove	Fridge
Dishwasher	Garden Tub	Stand-In Shower	Tub/Shower Combo
Walk-In Closet	Standard Closet	King Size Bedroom	Queen Size Bedroom
Computer Desk	Study	ADA compliant	Crown Molding
Gourmet Kitchen	Granite Counter Tops	Stainless Steel Appliances	Accent Walls

What activities are close to the apartment?

Light Rail	Bus Stop	Shopping	Night Life
Library	Arts	Hobby Shop	Movie Theater
Dance Classes	Fitness	Bakeries	Walking Trails
Camping	Boating	Sports Arenas	Parks
Skating	Skiing	Biking	Fishing

Apartment Stat Sheet

YES   NO

Name of Apartment _____

Phone (**)** _____ - _____   **Fax (**   **)** _____ - _____

Address _____

_____

Leasing Person's Name _____

How long are the leases?   MTM   3   4   5   6   7   8   9   10   11   12   13   14   15   16   17   18

Type _____ Sq Ft _____ $_____   Type _____ Sq Ft _____ $_____

Type _____ Sq Ft _____ $_____   Type _____ Sq Ft _____ $_____

Type _____ Sq Ft _____ $_____   Type _____ Sq Ft _____ $_____

Type _____ Sq Ft _____ $_____   Type _____ Sq Ft _____ $_____

Deposit $** _____ **Non Refundable Admin Fee$ _____ **Application Fee$** _____

Pet Deposit $ _____ **Non Refundable Pet Fee $** _____ **Pet Rent $** _____

Do they allow dogs? _____ **Do they allow cats?** _____ **What size?** _____ **How many?** _____

Does your pet qualify?   Y   N   **Exotic animals allowed?**   Y   N

___ Free Parking   ___ Uncovered   ___ Carport   ___ Closed-in Garage   ___ Garage Space

___ Street Parking   ___ Paid Lot Parking   **Monthly Cost $** _____

What are the utilities? What do you pay for?

____Water   ___Sewage   ___Trash   ___Electric   ___Gas   ___Cable/Dish TV   ___Phone

It is your responsibility to connect and disconnect your utilities. Be sure to ask which utilities you should place in your name. *Do not rely on your leasing person to make sure this gets done.* There could be a deposit to pay; the companies could pull your credit record again, although your utilities themselves will not be counted as credit. When you disconnect any service, ask for letters stating your payment history. Some companies in the future may use these letters so you might avoid a deposit another time.

Property Amenities Form

<u>Circle the amenities the property offers</u>

What amenities are offered in the community?

Tennis Court	Basketball Court	Sports Court	Handball Court
Volleyball Court	Swimming Pool	Hot Tub	Sauna
Steam Room	Yoga	Free Weights	Fitness Center
Massage Room	Dance Classes	Walking/Jogging Track	Theater Room
Daycare	Club House	Playground	Fire Pit
Tanning Bed	Barbecue Grills	Casino Trips	Concierge Service
Pet Walking Service	Personal Shopping	Dry Cleaning Service	Grocery Delivery

What amenities are in the home?

Fireplace	A/C	Self Cleaning Oven	Ice Maker
Microwave	DSL/T1 Cable	Stove	Fridge
Dishwasher	Garden Tub	Stand-In Shower	Tub/Shower Combo
Walk-In Closet	Standard Closet	King Size Bedroom	Queen Size Bedroom
Computer Desk	Study	ADA compliant	Crown Molding
Gourmet Kitchen	Granite Counter Tops	Stainless Steel Appliances	Accent Walls

What activities are close to the apartment?

Light Rail	Bus Stop	Shopping	Night Life
Library	Arts	Hobby Shop	Movie Theater
Dance Classes	Fitness	Bakeries	Walking Trails
Camping	Boating	Sports Arenas	Parks
Skating	Skiing	Biking	Fishing

Apartment Stat Sheet

YES   NO

Name of Apartment _____

Phone (_____ **)** _____ - _____   **Fax (** _____ **)** _____ - _____

Address _____

_____

Leasing Person's Name _____

How long are the leases?   MTM 3 4 5 6 7 8 9 10 11 12 13 14 15 16 17 18

Type _____ Sq Ft _____ $_____   Type _____ Sq Ft _____ $_____

Type _____ Sq Ft _____ $_____   Type _____ Sq Ft _____ $_____

Type _____ Sq Ft _____ $_____   Type _____ Sq Ft _____ $_____

Type _____ Sq Ft _____ $_____   Type _____ Sq Ft _____ $_____

Deposit $** _____ **Non Refundable Admin Fee$ _____ **Application Fee$** _____

Pet Deposit $ _____ **Non Refundable Pet Fee $** _____ **Pet Rent $** _____

Do they allow dogs? _____ **Do they allow cats?** _____ **What size?** _____ **How many?** _____

Does your pet qualify?   Y   N   **Exotic animals allowed?**   Y   N

___ Free Parking   ___ Uncovered   ___ Carport   ___ Closed-in Garage   ___ Garage Space

___ Street Parking   ___ Paid Lot Parking   **Monthly Cost $** _____

What are the utilities? What do you pay for?

____Water   ___Sewage   ___Trash   ___Electric   ___Gas   ___Cable/Dish TV   ___Phone

It is your responsibility to connect and disconnect your utilities. Be sure to ask which utilities you should place in your name. *Do not rely on your leasing person to make sure this gets done.* There could be a deposit to pay; the companies could pull your credit record again, although your utilities themselves will not be counted as credit. When you disconnect any service, ask for letters stating your payment history. Some companies in the future may use these letters so you might avoid a deposit another time.

Property Amenities Form

<u>Circle the amenities the property offers</u>

What amenities are offered in the community?

Tennis Court	Basketball Court	Sports Court	Handball Court
Volleyball Court	Swimming Pool	Hot Tub	Sauna
Steam Room	Yoga	Free Weights	Fitness Center
Massage Room	Dance Classes	Walking/Jogging Track	Theater Room
Daycare	Club House	Playground	Fire Pit
Tanning Bed	Barbecue Grills	Casino Trips	Concierge Service
Pet Walking Service	Personal Shopping	Dry Cleaning Service	Grocery Delivery

What amenities are in the home?

Fireplace	A/C	Self Cleaning Oven	Ice Maker
Microwave	DSL/T1 Cable	Stove	Fridge
Dishwasher	Garden Tub	Stand-In Shower	Tub/Shower Combo
Walk-In Closet	Standard Closet	King Size Bedroom	Queen Size Bedroom
Computer Desk	Study	ADA compliant	Crown Molding
Gourmet Kitchen	Granite Counter Tops	Stainless Steel Appliances	Accent Walls

What activities are close to the apartment?

Light Rail	Bus Stop	Shopping	Night Life
Library	Arts	Hobby Shop	Movie Theater
Dance Classes	Fitness	Bakeries	Walking Trails
Camping	Boating	Sports Arenas	Parks
Skating	Skiing	Biking	Fishing

Apartment Stat Sheet

YES   NO

Name of Apartment _____

Phone (**)** _____ - _____   **Fax (**   **)** _____ - _____

Address _____

_____

Leasing Person's Name _____

How long are the leases? **MTM 3 4 5 6 7 8 9 10 11 12 13 14 15 16 17 18**

Type _____ **Sq Ft** _____ **$** _____   **Type** _____ **Sq Ft** _____ **$** _____

Type _____ **Sq Ft** _____ **$** _____   **Type** _____ **Sq Ft** _____ **$** _____

Type _____ **Sq Ft** _____ **$** _____   **Type** _____ **Sq Ft** _____ **$** _____

Type _____ **Sq Ft** _____ **$** _____   **Type** _____ **Sq Ft** _____ **$** _____

Deposit $** _____ **Non Refundable Admin Fee$ _____ **Application Fee$** _____

Pet Deposit $ _____ **Non Refundable Pet Fee $** _____ **Pet Rent $** _____

Do they allow dogs? _____ **Do they allow cats?** _____ **What size?** _____ **How many?** _____

Does your pet qualify? **Y**   **N**   **Exotic animals allowed?** **Y**   **N**

___ Free Parking   ___Uncovered   ___ Carport   ___ Closed-in Garage   ___ Garage Space

___ Street Parking   ___Paid Lot Parking   **Monthly Cost $** _____

What are the utilities? What do you pay for?

____Water ___Sewage ___Trash ___Electric ___Gas ___Cable/Dish TV ___ Phone

It is your responsibility to connect and disconnect your utilities. Be sure to ask which utilities you should place in your name. *Do not rely on your leasing person to make sure this gets done.* There could be a deposit to pay; the companies could pull your credit record again, although your utilities themselves will not be counted as credit. When you disconnect any service, ask for letters stating your payment history. Some companies in the future may use these letters so you might avoid a deposit another time.

Property Amenities Form

<u>Circle the amenities the property offers</u>

What amenities are offered in the community?

Tennis Court	Basketball Court	Sports Court	Handball Court
Volleyball Court	Swimming Pool	Hot Tub	Sauna
Steam Room	Yoga	Free Weights	Fitness Center
Massage Room	Dance Classes	Walking/Jogging Track	Theater Room
Daycare	Club House	Playground	Fire Pit
Tanning Bed	Barbecue Grills	Casino Trips	Concierge Service
Pet Walking Service	Personal Shopping	Dry Cleaning Service	Grocery Delivery

What amenities are in the home?

Fireplace	A/C	Self Cleaning Oven	Ice Maker
Microwave	DSL/T1 Cable	Stove	Fridge
Dishwasher	Garden Tub	Stand-In Shower	Tub/Shower Combo
Walk-In Closet	Standard Closet	King Size Bedroom	Queen Size Bedroom
Computer Desk	Study	ADA compliant	Crown Molding
Gourmet Kitchen	Granite Counter Tops	Stainless Steel Appliances	Accent Walls

What activities are close to the apartment?

Light Rail	Bus Stop	Shopping	Night Life
Library	Arts	Hobby Shop	Movie Theater
Dance Classes	Fitness	Bakeries	Walking Trails
Camping	Boating	Sports Arenas	Parks
Skating	Skiing	Biking	Fishing

Apartment Stat Sheet

Name of Apartment _____

Phone (**)** _____ - _____   **Fax (**   **)** _____ - _____

Address _____

_____

Leasing Person's Name _____

How long are the leases?   MTM   3   4   5   6   7   8   9   10   11   12   13   14   15   16   17   18

Type _____ **Sq Ft** _____ **$** _____   **Type** _____ **Sq Ft** _____ **$** _____

Type _____ **Sq Ft** _____ **$** _____   **Type** _____ **Sq Ft** _____ **$** _____

Type _____ **Sq Ft** _____ **$** _____   **Type** _____ **Sq Ft** _____ **$** _____

Type _____ **Sq Ft** _____ **$** _____   **Type** _____ **Sq Ft** _____ **$** _____

Deposit $** _____ **Non Refundable Admin Fee$ _____ **Application Fee$** _____

Pet Deposit $ _____ **Non Refundable Pet Fee $** _____ **Pet Rent $** _____

Do they allow dogs? _____ **Do they allow cats?** _____ **What size?** _____ **How many?** _____

Does your pet qualify?   Y   N   **Exotic animals allowed?**   Y   N

___ Free Parking   ___Uncovered   ___ Carport   ___ Closed-in Garage   ___ Garage Space

___ Street Parking   ___Paid Lot Parking   **Monthly Cost $** _____

What are the utilities? What do you pay for?

____Water   ___Sewage   ___Trash   ___Electric   ___Gas   ___Cable/Dish TV   ___ Phone

It is your responsibility to connect and disconnect your utilities. Be sure to ask which utilities you should place in your name. *Do not rely on your leasing person to make sure this gets done.* There could be a deposit to pay; the companies could pull your credit record again, although your utilities themselves will not be counted as credit. When you disconnect any service, ask for letters stating your payment history. Some companies in the future may use these letters so you might avoid a deposit another time.

Property Amenities Form

<u>Circle the amenities the property offers</u>

What amenities are offered in the community?

Tennis Court	Basketball Court	Sports Court	Handball Court
Volleyball Court	Swimming Pool	Hot Tub	Sauna
Steam Room	Yoga	Free Weights	Fitness Center
Massage Room	Dance Classes	Walking/Jogging Track	Theater Room
Daycare	Club House	Playground	Fire Pit
Tanning Bed	Barbecue Grills	Casino Trips	Concierge Service
Pet Walking Service	Personal Shopping	Dry Cleaning Service	Grocery Delivery

What amenities are in the home?

Fireplace	A/C	Self Cleaning Oven	Ice Maker
Microwave	DSL/T1 Cable	Stove	Fridge
Dishwasher	Garden Tub	Stand-In Shower	Tub/Shower Combo
Walk-In Closet	Standard Closet	King Size Bedroom	Queen Size Bedroom
Computer Desk	Study	ADA compliant	Crown Molding
Gourmet Kitchen	Granite Counter Tops	Stainless Steel Appliances	Accent Walls

What activities are close to the apartment?

Light Rail	Bus Stop	Shopping	Night Life
Library	Arts	Hobby Shop	Movie Theater
Dance Classes	Fitness	Bakeries	Walking Trails
Camping	Boating	Sports Arenas	Parks
Skating	Skiing	Biking	Fishing

Apartment Stat Sheet

YES   NO

Name of Apartment _____

Phone (   ) _____ - _____   Fax (   ) _____ - _____

Address _____

_____

Leasing Person's Name_____

How long are the leases?   MTM   3   4   5   6   7   8   9   10   11   12   13   14   15   16   17   18

Type _____   Sq Ft _____ $_____   Type _____   Sq Ft _____ $_____

Type _____   Sq Ft _____ $_____   Type _____   Sq Ft _____ $_____

Type _____   Sq Ft _____ $_____   Type _____   Sq Ft _____ $_____

Type _____   Sq Ft _____ $_____   Type _____   Sq Ft _____ $_____

Deposit $ _____ Non Refundable Admin Fee$ _____ Application Fee$_____

Pet Deposit $ _____ Non Refundable Pet Fee $ _____ Pet Rent $_____

Do they allow dogs? _____ Do they allow cats? _____ What size? _____ How many? _____

Does your pet qualify?   Y   N   Exotic animals allowed?   Y   N

___ Free Parking   ___Uncovered   ___ Carport   ___ Closed-in Garage   ___ Garage Space

___ Street Parking   ___Paid Lot Parking   Monthly Cost $_____

What are the utilities?   What do you pay for?

____Water   ___Sewage   ___Trash   ___Electric   ___Gas   ___Cable/Dish TV   ___ Phone

It is your responsibility to connect and disconnect your utilities. Be sure to ask which utilities you should place in your name. *Do not rely on your leasing person to make sure this gets done.* There could be a deposit to pay; the companies could pull your credit record again, although your utilities themselves will not be counted as credit. When you disconnect any service, ask for letters stating your payment history. Some companies in the future may use these letters so you might avoid a deposit another time.

Property Amenities Form

<u>Circle the amenities the property offers</u>

What amenities are offered in the community?

Tennis Court	Basketball Court	Sports Court	Handball Court
Volleyball Court	Swimming Pool	Hot Tub	Sauna
Steam Room	Yoga	Free Weights	Fitness Center
Massage Room	Dance Classes	Walking/Jogging Track	Theater Room
Daycare	Club House	Playground	Fire Pit
Tanning Bed	Barbecue Grills	Casino Trips	Concierge Service
Pet Walking Service	Personal Shopping	Dry Cleaning Service	Grocery Delivery

What amenities are in the home?

Fireplace	A/C	Self Cleaning Oven	Ice Maker
Microwave	DSL/T1 Cable	Stove	Fridge
Dishwasher	Garden Tub	Stand-In Shower	Tub/Shower Combo
Walk-In Closet	Standard Closet	King Size Bedroom	Queen Size Bedroom
Computer Desk	Study	ADA compliant	Crown Molding
Gourmet Kitchen	Granite Counter Tops	Stainless Steel Appliances	Accent Walls

What activities are close to the apartment?

Light Rail	Bus Stop	Shopping	Night Life
Library	Arts	Hobby Shop	Movie Theater
Dance Classes	Fitness	Bakeries	Walking Trails
Camping	Boating	Sports Arenas	Parks
Skating	Skiing	Biking	Fishing

Apartment Stat Sheet

YES   NO

Name of Apartment _____

Phone (____ **)** _____ - _____   **Fax (** ____ **)** _____ - _____

Address _____

_____

Leasing Person's Name _____

How long are the leases?   MTM 3 4 5 6 7 8 9 10 11 12 13 14 15 16 17 18

Type _____ **Sq Ft** _____ **$** _____   **Type** _____ **Sq Ft** _____ **$** _____

Type _____ **Sq Ft** _____ **$** _____   **Type** _____ **Sq Ft** _____ **$** _____

Type _____ **Sq Ft** _____ **$** _____   **Type** _____ **Sq Ft** _____ **$** _____

Type _____ **Sq Ft** _____ **$** _____   **Type** _____ **Sq Ft** _____ **$** _____

Deposit $** _____ **Non Refundable Admin Fee$ _____ **Application Fee$** _____

Pet Deposit $ _____ **Non Refundable Pet Fee $** _____ **Pet Rent $** _____

Do they allow dogs? ____ **Do they allow cats?** ____ **What size?** ____ **How many?** _____

Does your pet qualify?   Y   N   **Exotic animals allowed?**   Y   N

___ Free Parking   ___Uncovered   ___ Carport   ___ Closed-in Garage   ___ Garage Space

___ Street Parking   ___Paid Lot Parking   **Monthly Cost $** _____

What are the utilities? What do you pay for?

____Water ___Sewage ___Trash ___Electric ___Gas ___Cable/Dish TV ___ Phone

It is your responsibility to connect and disconnect your utilities. Be sure to ask which utilities you should place in your name. *Do not rely on your leasing person to make sure this gets done.* There could be a deposit to pay; the companies could pull your credit record again, although your utilities themselves will not be counted as credit. When you disconnect any service, ask for letters stating your payment history. Some companies in the future may use these letters so you might avoid a deposit another time.

Property Amenities Form

Circle the amenities the property offers

What amenities are offered in the community?

Tennis Court	Basketball Court	Sports Court	Handball Court
Volleyball Court	Swimming Pool	Hot Tub	Sauna
Steam Room	Yoga	Free Weights	Fitness Center
Massage Room	Dance Classes	Walking/Jogging Track	Theater Room
Daycare	Club House	Playground	Fire Pit
Tanning Bed	Barbecue Grills	Casino Trips	Concierge Service
Pet Walking Service	Personal Shopping	Dry Cleaning Service	Grocery Delivery

What amenities are in the home?

Fireplace	A/C	Self Cleaning Oven	Ice Maker
Microwave	DSL/T1 Cable	Stove	Fridge
Dishwasher	Garden Tub	Stand-In Shower	Tub/Shower Combo
Walk-In Closet	Standard Closet	King Size Bedroom	Queen Size Bedroom
Computer Desk	Study	ADA compliant	Crown Molding
Gourmet Kitchen	Granite Counter Tops	Stainless Steel Appliances	Accent Walls

What activities are close to the apartment?

Light Rail	Bus Stop	Shopping	Night Life
Library	Arts	Hobby Shop	Movie Theater
Dance Classes	Fitness	Bakeries	Walking Trails
Camping	Boating	Sports Arenas	Parks
Skating	Skiing	Biking	Fishing

Apartment Stat Sheet

YES   NO

Name of Apartment _____

Phone (   ) _____ - _____   **Fax** (   ) _____ - _____

Address _____

_____

Leasing Person's Name _____

How long are the leases?   MTM   3   4   5   6   7   8   9   10   11   12   13   14   15   16   17   18

Type _____ **Sq Ft** _____ **$** _____   **Type** _____ **Sq Ft** _____ **$** _____

Type _____ **Sq Ft** _____ **$** _____   **Type** _____ **Sq Ft** _____ **$** _____

Type _____ **Sq Ft** _____ **$** _____   **Type** _____ **Sq Ft** _____ **$** _____

Type _____ **Sq Ft** _____ **$** _____   **Type** _____ **Sq Ft** _____ **$** _____

Deposit $** _____ **Non Refundable Admin Fee$ _____ **Application Fee$** _____

Pet Deposit $ _____ **Non Refundable Pet Fee $** _____ **Pet Rent $** _____

Do they allow dogs? _____ **Do they allow cats?** _____ **What size?** _____ **How many?** _____

Does your pet qualify?   Y   N   **Exotic animals allowed?**   Y   N

___ Free Parking   ___Uncovered   ___ Carport   ___ Closed-in Garage   ___ Garage Space

___ Street Parking   ___Paid Lot Parking   **Monthly Cost $** _____

What are the utilities? What do you pay for?

____Water   ___Sewage   ___Trash   ___Electric   ___Gas   ___Cable/Dish TV   ___ Phone

It is your responsibility to connect and disconnect your utilities. Be sure to ask which utilities you should place in your name. *Do not rely on your leasing person to make sure this gets done.* There could be a deposit to pay; the companies could pull your credit record again, although your utilities themselves will not be counted as credit. When you disconnect any service, ask for letters stating your payment history. Some companies in the future may use these letters so you might avoid a deposit another time.

Property Amenities Form

Circle the amenities the property offers

What amenities are offered in the community?

Tennis Court	Basketball Court	Sports Court	Handball Court
Volleyball Court	Swimming Pool	Hot Tub	Sauna
Steam Room	Yoga	Free Weights	Fitness Center
Massage Room	Dance Classes	Walking/Jogging Track	Theater Room
Daycare	Club House	Playground	Fire Pit
Tanning Bed	Barbecue Grills	Casino Trips	Concierge Service
Pet Walking Service	Personal Shopping	Dry Cleaning Service	Grocery Delivery

What amenities are in the home?

Fireplace	A/C	Self Cleaning Oven	Ice Maker
Microwave	DSL/T1 Cable	Stove	Fridge
Dishwasher	Garden Tub	Stand-In Shower	Tub/Shower Combo
Walk-In Closet	Standard Closet	King Size Bedroom	Queen Size Bedroom
Computer Desk	Study	ADA compliant	Crown Molding
Gourmet Kitchen	Granite Counter Tops	Stainless Steel Appliances	Accent Walls

What activities are close to the apartment?

Light Rail	Bus Stop	Shopping	Night Life
Library	Arts	Hobby Shop	Movie Theater
Dance Classes	Fitness	Bakeries	Walking Trails
Camping	Boating	Sports Arenas	Parks
Skating	Skiing	Biking	Fishing

Apartment Stat Sheet

YES   NO

Name of Apartment _____

Phone (_____ **)** _____ - _____   **Fax (** _____ **)** _____ - _____

Address _____

_____

Leasing Person's Name _____

How long are the leases?   MTM   3   4   5   6   7   8   9   10   11   12   13   14   15   16   17   18

Type _____ **Sq Ft** _____ **$**_____   **Type** _____ **Sq Ft** _____ **$**_____

Type _____ **Sq Ft** _____ **$**_____   **Type** _____ **Sq Ft** _____ **$**_____

Type _____ **Sq Ft** _____ **$**_____   **Type** _____ **Sq Ft** _____ **$**_____

Type _____ **Sq Ft** _____ **$**_____   **Type** _____ **Sq Ft** _____ **$**_____

Deposit $** _____ **Non Refundable Admin Fee$ _____ **Application Fee$**_____

Pet Deposit $ _____ **Non Refundable Pet Fee $** _____ **Pet Rent $**_____

Do they allow dogs? _____ **Do they allow cats?** _____ **What size?** _____ **How many?** _____

Does your pet qualify?   Y   N   **Exotic animals allowed?**   Y   N

___ Free Parking   ___Uncovered   ___ Carport   ___ Closed-in Garage   ___ Garage Space

___ Street Parking   ___ Paid Lot Parking   **Monthly Cost $**_____

What are the utilities? What do you pay for?

____Water   ___Sewage   ___Trash   ___Electric   ___Gas   ___Cable/Dish TV   ___ Phone

It is your responsibility to connect and disconnect your utilities. Be sure to ask which utilities you should place in your name. *Do not rely on your leasing person to make sure this gets done.* There could be a deposit to pay; the companies could pull your credit record again, although your utilities themselves will not be counted as credit. When you disconnect any service, ask for letters stating your payment history. Some companies in the future may use these letters so you might avoid a deposit another time.

Property Amenities Form

Circle the amenities the property offers

What amenities are offered in the community?

Tennis Court	Basketball Court	Sports Court	Handball Court
Volleyball Court	Swimming Pool	Hot Tub	Sauna
Steam Room	Yoga	Free Weights	Fitness Center
Massage Room	Dance Classes	Walking/Jogging Track	Theater Room
Daycare	Club House	Playground	Fire Pit
Tanning Bed	Barbecue Grills	Casino Trips	Concierge Service
Pet Walking Service	Personal Shopping	Dry Cleaning Service	Grocery Delivery

What amenities are in the home?

Fireplace	A/C	Self Cleaning Oven	Ice Maker
Microwave	DSL/T1 Cable	Stove	Fridge
Dishwasher	Garden Tub	Stand-In Shower	Tub/Shower Combo
Walk-In Closet	Standard Closet	King Size Bedroom	Queen Size Bedroom
Computer Desk	Study	ADA compliant	Crown Molding
Gourmet Kitchen	Granite Counter Tops	Stainless Steel Appliances	Accent Walls

What activities are close to the apartment?

Light Rail	Bus Stop	Shopping	Night Life
Library	Arts	Hobby Shop	Movie Theater
Dance Classes	Fitness	Bakeries	Walking Trails
Camping	Boating	Sports Arenas	Parks
Skating	Skiing	Biking	Fishing

Two Day Survival Kit:

Make bedroom and clothing boxes for each member of the family. Remember to put the name of whose box it is clearly on the outside of the box. Take these boxes over to your new home first. Place them in a hall closet with a sign on the door that states "Two Day Survival Kit".   This will remind you where you put the items while all your other household items are being delivered.

Box 1- Bathroom Supplies:

Bath soap	_____	Shaving razor	_____
Shampoo	_____	Tooth paste	_____
Tooth brush	_____	Toilet paper	_____
Four towels	_____	Four wash clothes	_____
Shower curtain	_____	Curtain rings	_____
Makeup case	_____	Blow dryer	_____
Brush	_____	Deodorant	_____
Medication	_____		

Box 2 - Kitchen Supplies:

Frying Pan	_____	Boiling Pan	_____
Paper Plates	_____	Baking Sheet	_____
Paper Cups	_____	Flat Ware	_____
Food for two days	_____		

Box 3- Clothing Supplies:

Undergarments	_____	Night Clothing	_____
Socks	_____	Shoes	_____
Shirts	_____	Pants	_____

Box 4 - Bedroom Supplies:

Pillows/Blanket	_____	Sheets	_____

Box 5 - Toolbox Supplies:

Hammer/Nails	_____	Garbage Bags	_____
Plier's	_____	Screw Driver	_____
Flashlight	_____	Paper/Pen	_____
Matches	_____		

Two Day Survival Kit:

Make bedroom and clothing boxes for each member of the family. Remember to put the name of whose box it is clearly on the outside of the box. Take these boxes over to your new home first. Place them in a hall closet with a sign on the door that states "Two Day Survival Kit". This will remind you where you put the items while all your other household items are being delivered.

Box 1- Bathroom Supplies:

Bath soap	_____	Shaving razor	_____
Shampoo	_____	Tooth paste	_____
Tooth brush	_____	Toilet paper	_____
Four towels	_____	Four wash clothes	_____
Shower curtain	_____	Curtain rings	_____
Makeup case	_____	Blow dryer	_____
Brush	_____	Deodorant	_____
Medication	_____		

Box 2 - Kitchen Supplies:

Frying Pan	_____	Boiling Pan	_____
Paper Plates	_____	Baking Sheet	_____
Paper Cups	_____	Flat Ware	_____
Food for two days	_____		

Box 3- Clothing Supplies:

Undergarments	_____	Night Clothing	_____
Socks	_____	Shoes	_____
Shirts	_____	Pants	_____

Box 4 - Bedroom Supplies:

Pillows/Blanket	_____	Sheets	_____

Box 5 - Toolbox Supplies:

Hammer/Nails	_____	Garbage Bags	_____
Plier's	_____	Screw Driver	_____
Flashlight	_____	Paper/Pen	_____
Matches	_____		

Two Day Survival Kit:

Make bedroom and clothing boxes for each member of the family. Remember to put the name of whose box it is clearly on the outside of the box. Take these boxes over to your new home first. Place them in a hall closet with a sign on the door that states "Two Day Survival Kit". This will remind you where you put the items while all your other household items are being delivered.

Box 1- Bathroom Supplies:

Bath soap	_____	Shaving razor	_____
Shampoo	_____	Tooth paste	_____
Tooth brush	_____	Toilet paper	_____
Four towels	_____	Four wash clothes	_____
Shower curtain	_____	Curtain rings	_____
Makeup case	_____	Blow dryer	_____
Brush	_____	Deodorant	_____
Medication	_____		

Box 2 - Kitchen Supplies:

Frying Pan	_____	Boiling Pan	_____
Paper Plates	_____	Baking Sheet	_____
Paper Cups	_____	Flat Ware	_____
Food for two days	_____		

Box 3- Clothing Supplies:

Undergarments	_____	Night Clothing	_____
Socks	_____	Shoes	_____
Shirts	_____	Pants	_____

Box 4 - Bedroom Supplies:

Pillows/Blanket	_____	Sheets	_____

Box 5 - Toolbox Supplies:

Hammer/Nails	_____	Garbage Bags	_____
Plier's	_____	Screw Driver	_____
Flashlight	_____	Paper/Pen	_____
Matches	_____		

<u>Two Day Survival Kit:</u>

Make bedroom and clothing boxes for each member of the family. Remember to put the name of whose box it is clearly on the outside of the box. Take these boxes over to your new home first. Place them in a hall closet with a sign on the door that states "Two Day Survival Kit". This will remind you where you put the items while all your other household items are being delivered.

Box 1- Bathroom Supplies:

Bath soap	_____	Shaving razor	_____
Shampoo	_____	Tooth paste	_____
Tooth brush	_____	Toilet paper	_____
Four towels	_____	Four wash clothes	_____
Shower curtain	_____	Curtain rings	_____
Makeup case	_____	Blow dryer	_____
Brush	_____	Deodorant	_____
Medication	_____		

Box 2 - Kitchen Supplies:

Frying Pan	_____	Boiling Pan	_____
Paper Plates	_____	Baking Sheet	_____
Paper Cups	_____	Flat Ware	_____
Food for two days	_____		

Box 3- Clothing Supplies:

Undergarments	_____	Night Clothing	_____
Socks	_____	Shoes	_____
Shirts	_____	Pants	_____

Box 4 - Bedroom Supplies:

Pillows/Blanket	_____	Sheets	_____

Box 5 - Toolbox Supplies:

Hammer/Nails	_____	Garbage bags	_____
Plier's	_____	Screw Driver	_____
Flashlight	_____	Paper/Pen	_____
Matches	_____		

TWO DAY

SURVIVAL KITS

ARE IN

THIS CLOSET.

PLACE NOTHING ELSE

IN HERE.

TWO DAY

SURVIVAL KITS

ARE IN

THIS CLOSET.

PLACE NOTHING ELSE

IN HERE.

Notes:_____

_____

_____

_____

_____

_____

_____

_____

_____

_____

_____

_____

_____

_____

_____

_____

_____

_____

_____

_____

_____

_____

_____

_____

_____

Notes:_____

_____

_____

_____

_____

_____

_____

_____

_____

_____

_____

_____

_____

_____

_____

_____

_____

_____

_____

_____

_____

_____

_____

_____

_____

_____

_____

_____

_____

Notes:_____

Notes:_____

_____

_____

_____

_____

_____

_____

_____

_____

_____

_____

_____

_____

_____

_____

_____

_____

_____

_____

_____

_____

_____

_____

_____

_____

_____

_____

_____

Notes:_____

_____

_____

_____

_____

_____

_____

_____

_____

_____

_____

_____

_____

_____

_____

_____

_____

_____

_____

_____

_____

_____

_____

_____

_____

_____

Notes:_____

_____

_____

_____

_____

_____

_____

_____

_____

_____

_____

_____

_____

_____

_____

_____

_____

_____

_____

_____

_____

_____

_____

_____

_____

_____

_____